IS-215: Unified Federal Review Advisory Training: An Overview of the UFR Process

By

Fema

8/22/2016

Lesson 1: Introduction and Course Overview

Course Welcome

This course is designed to help you understand Unified Federal Environmental and Historic Preservation Review (UFR) Process for environmental and historic preservation reviews for disaster recovery projects. This course will:

- Introduce the UFR Process.
- Describe the Tools and Mechanisms.
- Review stakeholders with whom the UFR Advisor may coordinate in the field.

This course is a prerequisite for obtaining the UFR Advisor specialty.

Course Structure

- This course is structured into 5 lessons and a course summary.
- To help you track your place within the course, the current lesson title will be displayed in the upper left corner of each screen. Also, a lesson list will be presented at the beginning and end of each lesson.
- This training is intended to be taken with the Student Manual available for additional explanations. Refer to the Student Manual for additional content to supplement slide text.

 This course should take approximately **2.5 hours** to complete. You must complete each lesson entirely to receive credit.

Lesson 1: Overview

We'll now continue with the content of the first lesson. This lesson presents:

- Course Objectives
- Screen Features
- Navigating Using Your Keyboard
- Receiving Credit

This lesson should take approximately **10 minutes** to complete.

Course Objectives

By the end of this course you should be able to:

- Describe the UFR Process and how it supports interagency coordination for EHP reviews during disaster recovery.
- Describe the UFR Advisor role in the UFR Process and its relationship to other disaster recovery positions.
- Explain what Tools and Mechanisms are available to implement the UFR Process.
- Explain when and how to use Tools and Mechanisms to implement the UFR Process during disaster recovery.

Screen Features

- Select the **Close** button to exit this window and access the menu listing all lessons of this course. You can select any of the lessons from this menu by simply selecting the lesson title.
- Select the **Glossary** button to look up key definitions and acronyms.
- Select the **Help** button to review guidance and troubleshooting advice regarding navigating through the course.
- Track your progress by looking at the **Progress** bar at the bottom of each screen.
- Follow the instructions that appear on each screen in order to proceed to the next screen or complete a Knowledge Review or Activity.
- Select the **Back** or the **Next** buttons at the bottom of screens to move backward or forward in the lesson. You may also use the "Navigation" panel located on the left side of the screen to navigate between pages and lessons. **Note**: If the **Next** button is **dimmed**, you must complete an activity before you can proceed in the lesson or use the left hand "Navigation" to bypass it.

Navigating Using Your Keyboard

Below are instructions for navigating through the course using your keyboard.

- Use the "Tab" key to move forward through each screen's navigation buttons and hyperlinks, or "Shift" + "Tab" to move backwards. A box surrounds the button that is currently selected. 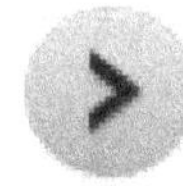
- Press "Enter" to select a navigation button or hyperlink.
- Use the arrow keys to select answers for multiple-choice review questions or self-assessment checklists. Then tab to the "Submit" 

button and press "Enter" to complete a Knowledge Review or Self-Assessment.

- **Warning:** Repeatedly pressing "Tab" beyond the number of selections on the screen may cause the keyboard to lock up. Use "Ctrl" + "Tab" to deselect an element or reset to the beginning of a screen's navigation links (most often needed for screens with animations or media).
- JAWS assistive technology users can press the "Ctrl" key to quiet the screen reader while the course audio plays.

Receiving Credit

To receive credit for this course, you must:

- **Complete all of the lessons.**

     It is important to allow enough time to complete the course in its entirety. Each lesson shows an approximate time to complete on the lesson's overview screen.
    Remember . . . YOU MUST COMPLETE THE ENTIRE COURSE TO RECEIVE CREDIT. If you must leave the course during your training, make note of the current location and use the **Navigation** found on the left hand side of the screen when you are ready to continue.
- **Pass the final exam.** The last screen provides instructions on how to complete the final exam.

Lesson 1 Summary

This lesson presented the following topics:

- Course Objectives
- Screen Features
- Navigating Using Your Keyboard
- Receiving Credit

↑ Back to Top

Lesson 2: The UFR Process and Interagency Coordination

Lesson 2: Overview

Objectives: This lesson will cover the following topics about the UFR Process:

- Foundations
- Integration with the National Disaster Recovery Framework
- Applicability
- Benefits

 This lesson should take approximately **30 minutes** to complete.

Statutory Authority

The Sandy Recovery Improvement Act of 2013 (SRIA)

Added Section 429 to the Stafford Act, directing the President, in consultation with DHS, FEMA, CEQ, and ACHP, to "establish an expedited and unified interagency review process to ensure compliance with environmental and historic requirements under federal law relating to disaster recovery projects, in order to expedite the recovery process, consistent with applicable law.

Click here to read Section 429 of the Stafford Act.

Oglala Sioux Tribal Leadership and FEMA dignitaries commemorate Federal Tribal Agreement signing (photo credit FEMA/Christopher Mardorf)

The UFR Process Established

An interagency MOU was executed by eleven departments and agencies on **July 29, 2014**, which committed them to support the UFR Process in the following ways:

- Provide staffing and resources.
- Distribute and use the Tools and Mechanisms and provide lessons learned and training to staff.

In addition, the MOU established an issue elevation process, to be followed as appropriate, to quickly resolve any issues or disputes that arise during the EHP review of a disaster recovery project.

Text description of image: Logo images of all eleven agencies that are signatories to the UFR MOU: 1-U.S. Department of Homeland Security, 2-United States of America Department of Energy, 3-U.S. Department of the Interior, 4-United States Environmental Protection Agency, 5-U.S. Department of Housing and Urban Development, 6-Executive Office of the President of the United States, 7-United States of America Department of Transportation, 8-United States Department of Agriculture, 9-Office of the Assistant Secretary of the Army, 10-Advisory Council on Historic Preservation, 11-United States of America Department of Commerce.

Interagency Oversight

The UFR Steering Group oversees the development and implementation of the UFR Process.

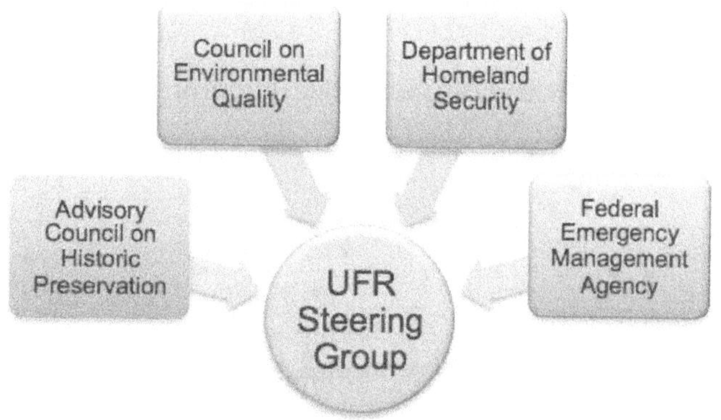

Text description of image: Diagram of the UFR Steering Group, surrounded by organizations that its membership represents: the Advisory Council on Historic Preservation, Council on Environmental Quality, Department of Homeland Security and Federal Emergency Management Agency.

The UFR Working Group assists in furthering development and implementation of the UFR Process.

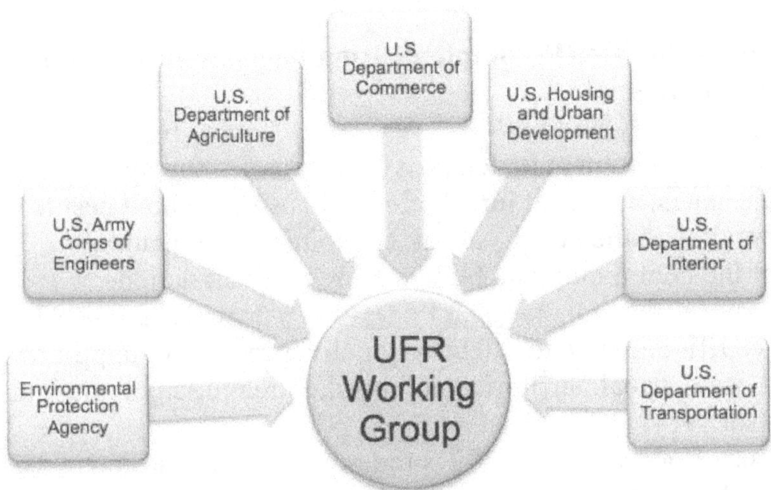

Text description of image: Diagram of the UFR Working Group, surrounded by federal agencies that its membership represents: Environmental Protection Agency, U.S. Army Corps of Engineers, U.S. Department of Agriculture, U.S. Department of Commerce, U.S. Housing and Urban Development, U.S. Department of Interior and U.S. Department of Transportation.

UFR Process Overview

What is the UFR Process?

- The UFR Process is a framework for coordinating federal agency EHP reviews for proposed disaster recovery projects associated with presidentially declared disasters under the Stafford Act.

What is the goal of the UFR Process?

- The purpose of the UFR Process is to improve federal decision making to allow for more timely and planned processes that yield better outcomes for communities and the environment when federal funds and permits are used for disaster recovery projects.

How do I implement the UFR Process?

- The UFR Process is implemented through educating stakeholders and using the Tools and Mechanisms, discussed in detail in Lesson 4.

UFR Integration with National Disaster Recovery Framework (NDRF)

The UFR Process integrates with the NDRF, complementing its goals and aligning with the NDRF organizational structure.

- The NDRF is the framework document which provides recovery support to disaster-impacted tribes, states, and local jurisdictions, focusing on how best to restore, redevelop and revitalize the health, social, economic, natural and environmental fabric of the community and build a more resilient nation.
- The Recovery Federal Interagency Operational Plan (FIOP) provides guidance on how to implement the NDRF and how to effectively deliver recovery support to disaster impacted local, state, tribal, territorial, and insular area jurisdictions. This includes the UFR Advisor.
- The Interagency Recovery Coordination (IRC) is the organizational structure as outlined in the Recovery FIOP, by which the federal government provides the appropriate level of needed support to the local, state, tribal, territorial, and insular area jurisdictions recovery efforts.
- Six Recovery Support Functions (RSFs) support the NDRF and can be activated, as needed.

More information on the NDRF can be found at this link.

UFR Advisor in the Context of the Federal Disaster Recovery Coordinator/ Recovery Support Function Management Structure

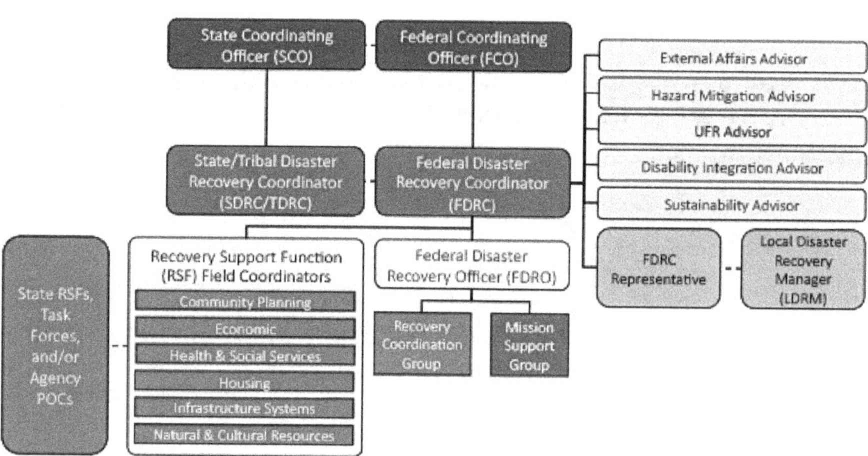

Click on each position/group for a description.

- State Coordinating Officer (SCO):
  - Appointed by the Governor to oversee the State's response and recovery efforts.
- Federal Coordinating Officer (FCO):
  - The FCO is the senior Federal official for response to and recovery from emergencies and major disasters. The FCO executes Stafford Act authorities, including commitment of FEMA resources and the issuance of mission assignments (MAs) to other Federal departments or agencies. The FCO is the primary Federal representative for Stafford Act events with whom the State/Tribal/Territorial Coordinating Officer (SCO/TCO) and other local, state, tribal, territorial, and insular area response officials interface to determine the most urgent needs and set objectives for an effective response.
- State/Tribal Disaster Recovery Coordinator (SDRC/TDRC):
  - The SDRC/TDRC organizes, coordinates, and advances recovery at the state, tribal, or territorial level. Their primary role is to manage and coordinate the redevelopment and building of their communities. The NDRF provides more information on the roles and responsibilities of the SDRC/TDRC.
- Federal Disaster Recovery Coordinator (FDRC):
  - The FDRC activates the RSFs and is the coordinating lead for RSF activities related to that specific disaster, and provides the leadership and direction that will guide RSF recovery activities. The FDRC supports the local, state, tribal, territorial, and insular area recovery goals set forth in the RSS. The FDRC will also support state, tribal, territorial, and insular area governments in building their recovery capacity after a disaster. When activated under the Stafford Act, the FDRC will function as a deputy to the FCO to coordinate Federal recovery efforts on the FCO's behalf during operations supporting Presidentially declared disasters.
- External Affairs Advisor:
  - The External Affairs Advisor works in support of the FCO and FDRC to ensure that accurate, actionable information is shared with all external recovery stakeholders, including: the general public and media; local, state, tribal, territorial, and insular area partners; the private sector; nongovernmental organizations; and members of Congress and their staff.
- Hazard Mitigation Advisor:
  - The Mitigation Advisor informs communities of opportunities to buy down risk throughout the recovery process. Mitigation Advisors are subject matter experts who are assigned to work across the RSFs as part of the NDRF, while advancing the principles of the National Mitigation Framework. The purpose of the FEMA Mitigation Advisor position is to bring broad mitigation expertise to the FDRC and all RSFs. The Mitigation Advisor demonstrates the benefits of mitigation and shows that it can be integrated without added time or significant effort by an RSF.

The Mitigation Advisor is the critical linkage to content, process, and internal and external networks, serving as an advisor to the FDRC on regional issues pertaining to recovery and mitigation.

- UFR Advisor:
  - The UFR Advisor is a field-level role, deployed as needed, to serve as the interagency coordinator for EHP compliance for disaster recovery projects in implementing the UFR Process.
- Disability Integration Advisor:
  - The Disability Integration Advisor at the JFO engages the disaster-affected community and also advises JFO staff on disability integration issues. In the community, the Disability Integration Advisor supports a network of local organizations that advocate for and provide services to people with disabilities and others with access and functional needs.
- Sustainability Advisor:
  - The Sustainability Advisor works to support the FDRC and is responsible for identifying opportunities to enhance and promote sustainability during disaster recovery.
- FDRC Representative:
  - The FDRC Representative is the state recovery counterpart to the FDRC and is responsible for organizing, coordinating, and advancing recovery at the state level. Their primary role is to manage and coordinate the recovery efforts in the state.
- Local Disaster Recovery Manager (LDRM):
  - The Local Disaster Recovery Manager (LDRM) organizes, coordinates, and advances recovery at the local level. Their primary role is to manage and coordinate the redevelopment and building of their communities.
- State RSFs, Task Forces, and/or Agency POCs:
  - State RSFs represent the equivalent state-level recovery framework that addresses housing, economic, environmental, infrastructure, and health and social services areas of assistance. State-led task forces represent state interests in particular recovery areas and include the Disaster Housing Task Force, which ensures the state's objectives and paths for post-disaster housing recovery are understood and integrated into the Federal recovery effort.
- Recovery Support Function (RSF) Field Coordinators:
  - The RSFs comprise the NDRF coordinating structure for key functional areas of assistance. The NDRF introduced six RSFs that provide structure to facilitate different issues and promote coordination among state and Federal agencies, nongovernmental partners, and stakeholders. Through these six RSFs, the Federal Government structures its support for assisting local, state, tribal, territorial, and insular area jurisdictions, the private sector, nonprofit agencies, voluntary agencies, and individuals in addressing recovery issues. RSFs are the primary, but not exclusive, Federal coordinating mechanisms for building, sustaining, and delivering the Recovery core capabilities. The RSFs serve to integrate interagency resources and support the development and implementation of the RSS.

RSFs are not based on the capabilities of a single department or agency but represent groups of organizations that work together to deliver core capabilities and support effective recovery operations.

- Federal Disaster Recovery Officer (FDRO):
    - The FDRO's role is to assist the FDRC in the execution of the Recovery Coordination mission, coordination of the assessment processes, and development and implementation of the RSS by providing general operational and management support.
- Recovery Coordination Group:
    - This group at the JFO is managed by the FDRC and supports the recovery coordination organization by establishing and managing coordination structures with all recovery stakeholders to include RSF Field Coordinators, FEMA Program Areas, governmental partners, and the private sector to identify and leverage recovery resources, policies, and programs. The Recovery Coordination Group enhances coordination and collaboration through facilitating discussions and information/data sharing, which supports recovery efforts. This group will be staffed by personnel from FEMA's NDRS Cadre.
- Mission Support Group:
    - This group supports the FDRC's effort to develop community-based, interagency, and partnership outreach and communication approaches with local, state, tribal, territorial, and insular area partners. (This is distinct from the ESF #15 [External Affairs] mission to provide public information.) The group maintains the efficiency and productivity of the organization by providing mission administrative support, managing all human resources activities, and helping to coordinate Interagency Agreements (IAAs) and MAs. This group is generally staffed by FEMA's National Disaster Recovery Support (NDRS) Cadre.

More information is available in Lesson 3 on how the UFR Advisor interacts and coordinates with some of the positions and groups displayed above.

When is the UFR Process Applicable?

- The UFR Process is used when multiple agencies are engaged in the same presidentially-declared disaster recovery effort.
- The UFR Process applies whether or not a UFR Advisor is activated in the field.
- The UFR Process applies whether or not the RSFs are activated or FDRC is appointed.
- The FEMA EHP Advisor and Federal EHP Practitioners should be familiar with and know how to apply Tools and Mechanisms even if the UFR Advisor is not activated.
- The Tools and Mechanisms can be used in any situation to improve interagency coordination.

Lesson 5 presents two examples of how the UFR Process can be applied.

UFR Process During Disaster Recovery

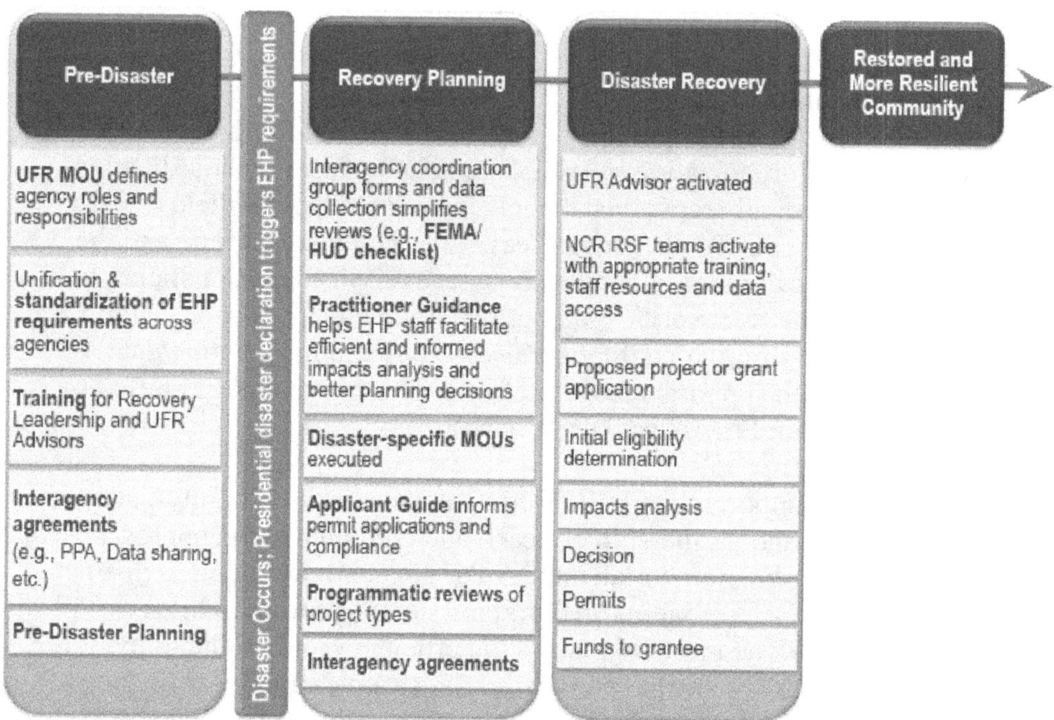

Text description of image: Timeline of the UFR Process during the phases of disaster recovery. The five phases are: 1) Pre-Disaster, 2) Disaster Occurs, 3) Recovery Planning, 4) Disaster Recovery, 5) Restored and More Resilient Community. During the Pre-Disaster phase, the following takes place: UFR MOU defines agency roles and responsibilities; Unification & standardization of EHP requirements across agencies; Training for Recovery Leadership and UFR Advisors; Interagency agreements (e.g., PPA, Data sharing, etc.); and Pre-Disaster Planning. When the disaster occurs, a Presidential disaster declaration triggers EHP requirements. During Recovery Planning, the following takes place: Interagency coordination group forms and data collection simplifies reviews (e.g., FEMA/HUD checklist); Practitioner Guidance helps EHP staff facilitate efficient and informed impacts analysis and better planning decisions; Disaster-specific MOUs executed; Applicant Guide informs permit applications and compliance; Programmatic reviews of project types; Interagency agreements. During Disaster Recovery, the following takes place: UFR Advisor activated; NCR RSF teams activate with appropriate training, staff resources and data access; Proposed project or grant application; Initial eligibility determination; Impacts analysis; Decision; Permits; Funds to grantee.

Benefits of the UFR Process

The UFR Process improves federal decision making to allow for more timely and integrated processes, resulting in better outcomes for communities and the environment when federal funds and permits are used for disaster recovery projects.

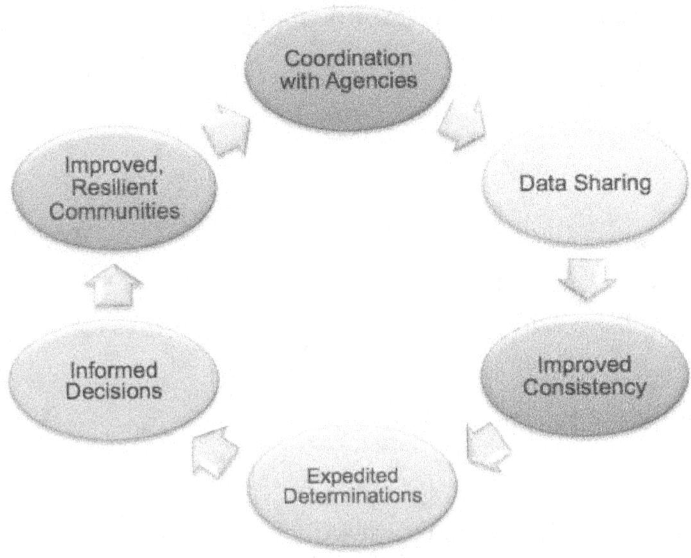

How Can the UFR Process Assist Agencies?

UFR Process can assist agencies to:	**UFR Process is not intended to:**
Create opportunities for greater coordination across agencies to expedite EHP requirements.	Circumvent or supersede any existing federal, tribal, state, or local EHP requirements.
Strive to reduce duplication of information provided by applicants working with multiple agencies.	Eliminate requirements for consultations between agencies and between agencies and applicants.
Leverage existing and develop new interagency agreements, such as MOUs and programmatic agreements.	Change existing interagency agreements.
Align review processes and prepare joint reviews with other agencies to satisfy one or more EHP requirements.	Establish a single review process for agencies funding a single project.

For More Information

The UFR Webpage is a one stop source for information about the UFR Process. It contains Tools and Mechanisms such as:

- UFR Guidance for EHP Practitioners (Practitioner Guidance), including Tools and Mechanisms in the Appendices
- Unified Federal Environmental and Historic Preservation Review Guide for Federal Disaster Recovery Assistance Applicants (Applicant Guide)
- UFR Newsletter
- Best Practices Library
- and much more…

To access the UFR Webpage, click here.

Lesson 2 Summary

This lesson presented the following topics about the UFR Process:

- Foundations
- Integration with the National Disaster Recovery Framework
- Applicability
- Benefits

Lesson 3: The UFR Advisor

Lesson 3: Overview

Objectives: This lesson will cover the following topics about the UFR Advisor:

- Qualifications
- Activation and deactivation
- Role and responsibilities
- Context in the disaster recovery process
- Relationship to other disaster recovery positions

 This lesson should take approximately **40 minutes** to complete.

How Do FEMA EHP Staff Qualify to Serve as UFR Advisors?

- Complete this training.
- Obtain a letter of recommendation from your Regional Environmental Officer (REO) or cadre coordinator, or, if you are the REO, from your Division Director, which demonstrates your ability to work and coordinate with multiple federal agencies during disaster recovery operations.
- Personnel applying for this specialty should submit their request to FEMA's Office of Environmental and Historic Preservation certifying official.

When Might I be Activated? (FDRC Scenario)

If an FDRC is appointed:

- The UFR Advisor is activated to the field to conduct a UFR Advisor Mission Scoping Assessment (UFR MSA). This assessment determines whether there are UFR opportunities for the UFR Advisor. This person reports directly to the FDRC.
- Typically, the Regional UFR Coordinator will activate as the UFR Advisor, unless they are already engaged in other disaster recovery operations.
- The UFR Advisor activation schedule is flexible and depends on disaster-specific requirements. Usually, within a few days of the disaster, monitoring and situational awareness and the Advance Evaluation occur. Within a few weeks, the FDRC is appointed, RSFs are activated, and the UFR Advisor is activated to conduct the UFR MSA. Within a month, the National UFR Coordinator is notified.

How Does My Role Fit in the Disaster Recovery Process?

Scenario: The RSFs are activated and the FDRC is appointed.

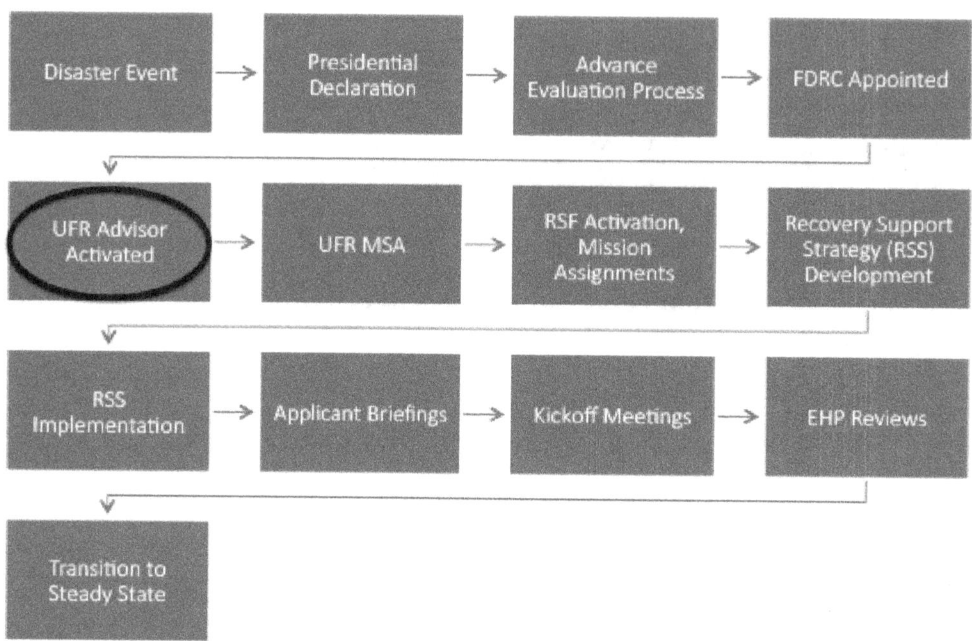

Text description of this image: Flow chart depicting the sequence of the disaster recovery process. Steps are as follows: 1) Disaster Event; 2) Presidential Declaration; 3) Advance Evaluation Process; 4) FDRC Appointed; 5) UFR Advisor Activated; 6) UFR MSA; 7) RSF Activation, Mission Assignments; 8) Recovery Support Strategy (RSS) Development; 9) RSS Implementation; 10) Applicant Briefings; 11) Kickoff Meetings; 12) EHP Reviews; and 13) Transition to Steady State.

Click on each operational milestone on the figure to learn more about it.

- **Advance Evaluation Process**
  - Description: If the Regional Administrator or FCO needs additional information to help determine whether the activation of an FDRC is warranted, the FCO can call upon an Advance Evaluation Team (AET) to conduct a rapid initial assessment. The AET assists the FCO to determine if activation of an FDRC is warranted, provides initial recommendation on potential RSF activation and provides insight of potential recovery issues and challenges.
  - UFR Advisor Activities: n/a
- **FDRC Appointed**
  - Description: Once the FDRC is appointed, the FDRC will engage the NDRPD, RSF National coordinators, FEMA Regions, JFO elements, and RSF contacts at the regional level to provide situational awareness.

- o UFR Advisor Activities: n/a
- **UFR Advisor Activated**
  - o Description: UFR Advisor activates to the JFO.
  - o UFR Advisor Activities:
    - Identify meetings and task forces to join in coordination with the FDRC or chief of staff/FCO, EHP Advisor and REO.
    - Coordinate with other funding agencies.
    - Establish communication with RSFs under the NDRF, if applicable.
- **UFR MSA**
  - o Description: This assessment summarizes the key challenges and issues and is used to develop the Recovery Support Strategy (RSS).
  - o UFR Advisor Activities:
    - In coordination with the EHP Advisor, and REO when appropriate, determine resource/regulatory agencies to engage.
    - Gather data to identify EHP compliance priorities and needs, including needs for additional resources through mission assignments and RSFs.
    - Determine additional funding agencies to engage.
    - Encourage EHP Practitioners to build interagency relationships and pre-position resources and analyses in advance of EHP compliance.
- **RSF Activation and Mission Assignments**
  - o Description: RSFs are activated by the FDRC. The FDRC may activate all RSFs or select RSFs when significant impacts to particular sectors of the community are reported. The FCO determines what Mission Assignments (deployment of federal agency expertise and resources to state and local governments) are necessary to support response and recovery.
  - o UFR Advisor Activities: n/a
- **Recovery Support Strategy (RSS) Development**
  - o Description: The Recovery Support Strategy (RSS) provides a unified strategy or approach of the FDRC-RSF operation and describes specific steps that the FDRC and RSF agencies will use to support recovery needs.
  - o UFR Advisor Activities: Identify specific UFR strategies and agreements for inclusion in the Mission Scoping Assessment and Recovery Support Strategy.
- **RSS Implementation**
  - o Description: Implementation of the strategy and protocols in the RSS.
  - o UFR Advisor Activities: Advise FDRC and EHP Practitioners in the implementation of the UFR Process.
- **Applicant Briefings**
  - o Description: Meetings held by the state to inform prospective applicants of available assistance and eligibility requirements for obtaining federal assistance under the declared event.
  - o UFR Advisor Activities:

- Reach out to states, tribes and other applicants in coordination with the EHP Advisor and REO to build awareness and transparency with EHP compliance.
    - Participate, to the extent practicable, in applicant briefings.
- **Kickoff Meetings**
  - Description: Meetings held to facilitate information exchange between FEMA and applicants for federal assistance.
  - UFR Advisor Activities:
    - Encourage interagency attendance at FEMA-led meeting.
    - Encourage distribution of Tools and Mechanisms, including the Applicant Guide and web-based tools on the UFR Webpage.
- **EHP reviews: including the scoping, consultation and analysis**
  - Description: Funding applications are reviewed for compliance with EHP requirements.
  - UFR Advisor Activities:
    - Serve as Point of Contact for JFO and/or recovery office re: UFR Process.
    - Coordinate with the EHP Advisor, National UFR Coordinator and REO regarding JFO and/or recovery office activities.
    - Serve as advisor to the FDRC or chief of staff/FCO for interagency EHP issues.
    - Participate in scoping meetings with resource agencies, and discuss the anticipated consultation processes and efficiencies that may be applied.
    - Develop working groups for major recovery issues for EHP compliance, such as debris, to develop efficiencies.
    - Coordinate with RSFs, including NCR RSF, to identify ways to fill resource gaps.
    - Maintain coordination with tribes, State Historic Preservation Officers, state and local environmental offices, field coordinators, funding and resource agencies (including mission assigned staff) for EHP compliance.
    - Provide status updates to REO and National UFR Coordinator.
    - Encourage EHP Practitioners to leverage existing analyses, permits, agreements and tools to expedite reviews.
    - Contribute to after action reports and other documentation of UFR implementation and EHP compliance.
- **Transition to Steady State**
  - Description: Demobilization and transition of to steady state operations. This does not necessarily signify the end of the recovery support mission.
  - UFR Advisor Activities: Contribute to after action reports and other documentation of UFR implementation and EHP compliance.

The UFR Advisor's Relationship to Other Disaster Recovery Positions

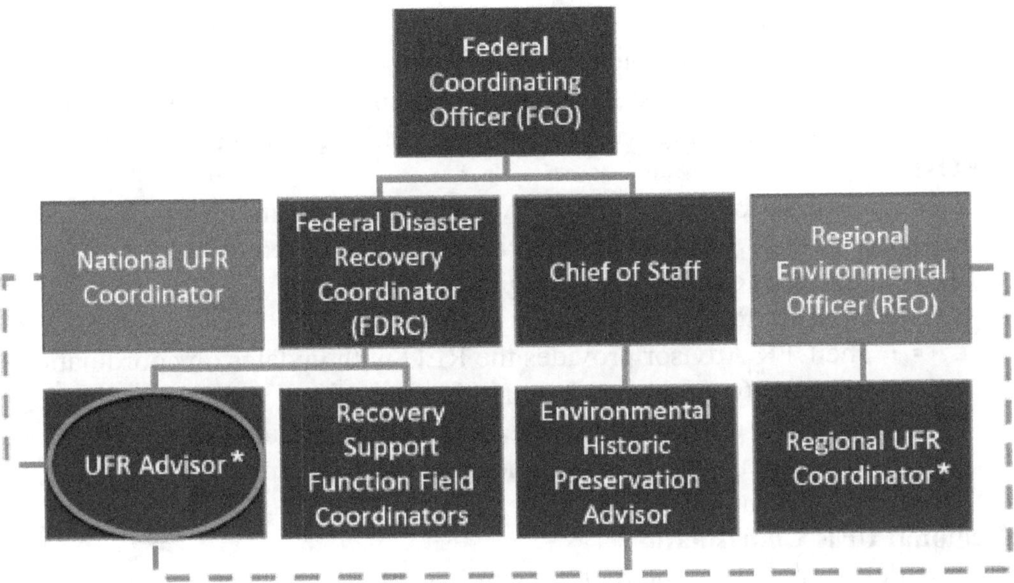

UFR Advisor Coordination Structure

Click each other disaster recovery position to learn more about other parties involved in EHP reviews and the various ways in which the UFR Advisor interacts with them.

- **The Federal disaster recovery leadership (FDRCs, FCOs, and Chiefs of Staff):**
    - Oversees activities at the JFO and/or recovery office.
    - **Relationship to the UFR Advisor:**
        - If the FDRC is appointed, a UFR Advisor will activate.
        - The UFR Advisor supports the FDRC/FCO mission by encouraging the RSF Field Coordinators and agencies when possible, to front-load EHP information into project planning, so that states and communities can quickly recover while complying with appropriate EHP regulations.
        - The UFR Advisor identifies and supports the development of EHP efficiencies so that states and communities can quickly recover while complying with appropriate EHP regulations.
- **The National UFR Coordinator:**
    - Provides oversight for the implementation of the UFR Process.
    - Supports the FDRC.
    - Tracks UFR Process implementation and provides recommendations for future needs.
    - Attends Recovery Support Functions Leadership Group (RSFLG) Meetings.
    - **Relationship to the UFR Advisor:**
        - The UFR Advisor supports the FDRC/FCO mission by encouraging the RSF Field Coordinators and agencies when

possible, to front-load EHP information into project planning, so that states and communities can quickly recover while complying with appropriate EHP regulations.

  - The UFR Advisor identifies and supports the development of EHP efficiencies so that states and communities can quickly recover while complying with appropriate EHP regulations.

- **The REOs:**
  - Are responsible for directing FEMA's EHP Program in the region.
  - Have expert knowledge of regional issues and EHP requirements.
  - Have established contacts in the region.
  - **Relationship to the UFR Advisor:**
    - The UFR Advisor provides the REO with updates on coordination activities (e.g., through reports, best practices, and contact lists) and seeks guidance from the REO and Regional UFR Coordinator on appropriate parties and methods of engagement for agencies and stakeholders.

- **The Regional UFR Coordinator:**
  - Provides oversight for the regional implementation of the UFR Process.
  - Identifies opportunities for regional interagency coordination and cooperation for the REO.
  - Tracks EHP review efficiencies related to disaster recovery projects.
  - Is active during pre-disaster planning.
  - **Relationship to the UFR Advisor:**
    - Typically, the Regional UFR Coordinator will activate as the UFR Advisor, unless they are already engaged in other disaster recovery operations.
    - The UFR Advisor seeks guidance from the Regional UFR Coordinator as needed, reports coordination activities accomplished at the JFO and/or recovery office to the Regional UFR Coordinator.
    - The Regional UFR Coordinator completes outstanding EHP compliance issues following the transition back to the regions after JFO and/or recovery office closure.

- **The RSF Field Coordinators:**
  - When RSFs are activated, RSF Field Coordinators support the FDRC virtually or on site by providing expertise.
  - RSF Field Coordinators are staff volunteers who are mission-assigned to the JFO to facilitate the identification, coordination and delivery of Federal assistance needed to supplement recovery resources and efforts by local, State and Tribal governments, as well as private and nonprofit sectors.
  - The six RSFs are Community Planning and Capacity Building, Health and Social Services, Infrastructure Systems, Economic, Housing, and Natural and Cultural Resources.
  - **Relationship to the UFR Advisor:**

- The UFR Advisor coordinates with all activated RSF Field Coordinators to leverage resources and expertise, ensuring that EHP compliance considerations are integrated into project planning and recovery efforts.
- **The EHP Advisor:**
  - Is responsible for **EHP compliance** for FEMA-funded projects, establishing and directing a disaster incident's EHP program and ensuring its functional integration into the FEMA mission.
  - Provides advice and assistance in carrying out the EHP functions in the incident, including compliance with FEMA's EHP regulations and procedures.
  - Implements the Tools and Mechanisms if UFR Advisor is not activated.
  - **Relationship to the UFR Advisor:**
    - The UFR Advisor enhances the capabilities of, and works closely with, the EHP Advisor by supporting interagency coordination. The UFR Advisor shares information with the EHP Advisor about EHP compliance, coordination and anticipated issues. The UFR Advisor also recommends interagency and programmatic approaches to FEMA's EHP compliance and assists the EHP Advisor with interagency coordination for projects.

UFR Advisor Mission Scoping Assessment

If an FDRC is appointed, the UFR Advisor activates for approximately 30 days and will develop the UFR Advisor Mission Scoping Assessment (UFR MSA) that identifies UFR opportunities and scopes their mission for the disaster. The UFR Advisor will use the template UFR MSA to develop the document, which contains criteria for the UFR Advisor to assess if there is a UFR mission.

- The UFR MSA will provide a recommendation on whether the UFR Advisor will remain activated beyond the initial 30 day period. The decision to discontinue the UFR Advisor's activation allows for reassessments in the future if additional agencies or funding is made available.
- The UFR MSA will be submitted to the National UFR Coordinator and to the FDRC.

What is the Role of the UFR Advisor?

The UFR Advisor:

- Serves as the **interagency coordinator** for EHP compliance for disaster recovery projects.

- Supports Disaster Recovery Leadership.
- Identifies opportunities for EHP efficiencies
- Consults the National and Regional UFR Coordinators.
- Works closely with the FEMA EHP Advisor.
- Coordinates with RSF Field Coordinators.
- Updates, seeks guidance from, and coordinates with the FEMA REO.

What Are the Core Duties as UFR Advisor?

The UFR Advisor serves as the interagency coordinator for EHP compliance. In this role, the UFR Advisor:

- Educates staff and interagency partners about the UFR Process.
- Recommends specific Tools and Mechanisms to be used to support disaster recovery and facilitates their development.
- Acts as liaison between federal agencies to identify opportunities to expedite EHP compliance and promote interagency coordination.
- Facilitates coordination meetings across agencies (including federal, tribal, state and local) leveraging existing meetings or scheduling new meetings.
- Coordinates federal technical assistance capabilities to support EHP reviews.

EHP Roles in Disaster Recovery

UFR Advisor

- **Mission:** Interagency EHP Coordination
- **Reports to:** FDRC
- **Activated:** If an FDRC is appointed (Stafford Act only)
- Build relationships with stakeholders and federal agencies.
- Communicate relevant EHP information to stakeholders and federal agencies.
- Determine opportunities for coordination in

FEMA EHP Advisor

- **Mission:** FEMA EHP Compliance
- **Reports to:** FCO
- **Activated:** Most Stafford Act events
- Identify the level of EHP review required for a FEMA project.
- Assist with consultations or permits, if necessary, for FEMA projects.
- Build relationships with stakeholders and federal agencies.
- Communicate relevant EHP

NCR RSF

- **Mission:** Assist states and tribes with long-term environmental and cultural resource recovery planning
- **Reports to:** FDRC
- **Activated:** If an AET determines necessary, Stafford Act or non-Stafford Act
- Gather data on natural and historic resources in the disaster area.
- Develop a pre-disaster NCR RSF

meeting EHP requirements.
- Identify and develop programmatic solutions for interagency efficiencies.

information to FEMA applicants.
- Identify and develop programmatic options for meeting FEMA regulatory obligations.

action plan to identify and communicate priority actions.
- Promote the principles of sustainable and disaster resilient communities through the protection of natural resources.

Are There Additional Parties Involved in EHP Reviews?

In coordinating and expediting EHP reviews for disaster recovery projects, the UFR Advisor will also interact with the following parties.

Party	Party Description	UFR advisor's Interaction
EHP Practitioners	Agency staff responsible for conducting or contributing to EHP reviews, including HUD responsible entities under HUD's Community Development Block Grant Program	Encourages EHP Practitioners to build interagency relationships and advises them on implementing UFR aspects of the Recovery Support Strategy
Applicants	Organizations or governments who apply for direct federal funding or assistance	Builds transparency and awareness of EHP compliance
Other Government Entities	Tribal, state, and/or local government representatives	Maintains coordination throughout EHP scoping, consultation, and analysis

When Might I be Activated? (Non-FDRC Scenario)

If an FDRC is not appointed:

- An EHP Advisor, in charge of FEMA's EHP compliance, may assume some of responsibilities for implementing the UFR Process. Those responsibilities include:
    - Identification and use of appropriate UFR Tools and Mechanisms to expedite EHP reviews
    - Identification and development of EHP efficiencies; and
    - Sharing of EHP data and resources and interagency coordination.

- If an EHP Advisor identifies a need for assistance for coordinating a FEMA-funded project with another agency, an EHP cadre member with the UFR specialty may be activated to support the EHP Advisor.
- If activated, the EHP cadre member will report directly to the EHP Advisor.

How Does My Role Fit in the Disaster Recovery Process?

Scenario: The RSFs have not been activated and the FDRC is not appointed.

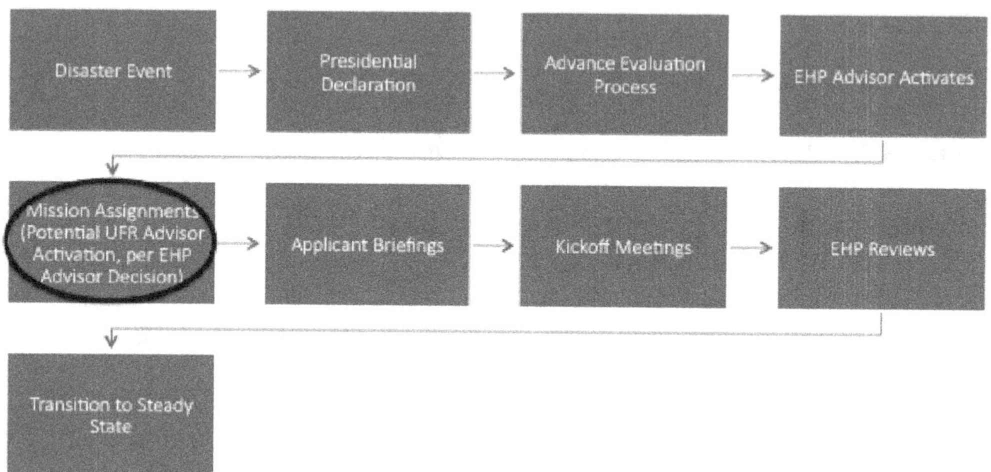

Text description of this image: Flow chart depicting the sequence of the disaster recovery process. Steps are as follows: 1) Disaster Event; 2) Presidential Declaration; 3) Advance Evaluation Process; 4) EHP Advisor Activates; 5) Mission Assignments (Potential UFR Advisor Activation, per EHP Advisor Decision); 6) Applicant Briefings; 7) Kickoff Meetings; 8) EHP Reviews; and 9) Transition to Steady State.

Click on each operational milestone on the figure to learn more about it.

- **Advance Evaluation Process**
    - Description: If the Regional Administrator or FCO needs additional information to help determine whether the activation of an FDRC is warranted, the FCO can call upon an Advance Evaluation Team (AET) to conduct a rapid initial assessment. The AET assists the FCO to determine if activation of an FDRC is warranted, provides initial recommendation on potential RSF activation and provides insight of potential recovery issues and challenges.
    - UFR Advisor Activities: n/a
- **Mission Assignments (Potential UFR Advisor Activation, per EHP Advisor Decision)**
    - Description: If the EHP Advisor determines that there is a UFR Advisor mission, the UFR Advisor activates to the JFO.
    - UFR Advisor Activities:

- Identify meetings and task forces to join in coordination with the EHP Advisor and REO.
    - Coordinate with other funding agencies.
- **Applicant Briefings**
    - Description: Meetings held by the state to inform prospective applicants of available assistance and eligibility requirements for obtaining federal assistance under the declared event.
    - UFR Advisor Activities:
        - Reach out to states, tribes and other applicants in coordination with the EHP Advisor and REO to build awareness and transparency with EHP compliance.
        - Participate, to the extent practicable, in applicant briefings.
- **Kickoff Meetings**
    - Description: Meetings held to facilitate information exchange between FEMA and applicants for federal assistance.
    - UFR Advisor Activities:
        - Encourage interagency attendance at FEMA-led meeting.
        - Encourage distribution of Tools and Mechanisms, including the Applicant Guide and web-based tools on the UFR Webpage.
- **EHP reviews: including the scoping, consultation and analysis**
    - Description: Funding applications are reviewed for compliance with EHP requirements.
    - UFR Advisor Activities:
        - Serve as Point of Contact for JFO and/or recovery office re: UFR Process.
        - Coordinate with the EHP Advisor, National UFR Coordinator and REO regarding JFO and/or recovery office activities.
        - Serve as advisor to the FDRC or chief of staff/FCO for interagency EHP issues.
        - Participate in scoping meetings with resource agencies, and discuss the anticipated consultation processes and efficiencies that may be applied.
        - Develop working groups for major recovery issues for EHP compliance, such as debris, to develop efficiencies.
        - Coordinate with RSFs, including NCR RSF, to identify ways to fill resource gaps.
        - Maintain coordination with tribes, State Historic Preservation Officers, state and local environmental offices, field coordinators, funding and resource agencies (including mission assigned staff) for EHP compliance.
        - Provide status updates to REO and National UFR Coordinator.
        - Encourage EHP Practitioners to leverage existing analyses, permits, agreements and tools to expedite reviews.
        - Contribute to after action reports and other documentation of UFR implementation and EHP compliance.
- **Transition to Steady State**

- o Description: Demobilization and transition of to steady state operations.
    This does not necessarily signify the end of the recovery support mission.
  - o UFR Advisor Activities: Contribute to after action reports and other
    documentation of UFR implementation and EHP compliance.

Roles and Responsibilities of EHP Cadre Staff

Once activated, the EHP cadre staff member will assist the EHP Advisor in the following
ways:

- Development and implementation of Tools and Mechanisms, such as a disaster-
  specific memorandum of understanding (MOU).
- Support identification of data sharing opportunities and facilitate development of
  data sharing agreements to encourage unified data use for FEMA.
- Support the EHP Advisor, FEMA's interagency coordinator for EHP compliance,
  by:
  - o Helping identify and facilitate meetings across agencies to share EHP
    compliance information and prioritize/coordinate the implementation of
    FEMA interagency EHP actions and strategies.
  - o Supporting the EHP Advisor as they act as a liaison between FEMA and
    other federal agencies at the JFO and/or recovery office to identify
    opportunities to expedite FEMA's EHP compliance and promote
    unification during disaster recovery and encourage interagency
    engagement at the regional level with the REO and counterparts at other
    federal agencies.
  - o Supporting the EHP Advisor for outreach to tribes and other stakeholders
    and to understand the breadth and scope of FEMA's EHP responsibilities
    at each disaster.
  - o Supporting the EHP Advisor's coordination with the region to keep the
    REO informed of EHP compliance issues and UFR Process activities.

When Long Will I be Activated?

- The length of activation will vary depending on need.
- If the UFR Advisor is still active when the JFO closes, the UFR Advisor may be
  demobilized or transitioned to the region depending on need.
- If the UFR Advisor is still active when the JFO transitions to a recovery office,
  the UFR Advisor may be demobilized or transitioned to the recovery office.

Lesson 3 Summary

This lesson presented the following topics:

- Qualifications
- Activation and deactivation
- Role and responsibilities
- Context in the disaster recovery process
- Relationship to other disaster recovery positions

Lesson 4: Tools and Mechanisms of the UFR Process

Lesson 4: Overview

Objectives: This lesson will cover the following topics about the Tools and Mechanisms:

- Detailed descriptions
- UFR Advisor's role in implementation
- Benefits for disaster recovery

 This lesson should take approximately **30 minutes** to complete.

UFR Process - Tools and Mechanisms

- The UFR Process encourages EHP Practitioners to use the **Tools and Mechanisms** to expedite EHP reviews by addressing gaps in EHP review processes, increasing consistency, and leveraging existing resources to create process efficiencies.
- Tools are products that support the UFR Process while Mechanisms are the processes for implementing a unified and expedited EHP review for disaster recovery projects.
- The Tools and Mechanisms promote best practices that improve efficiency and information sharing within existing regulatory requirements for EHP reviews.

What are the Tools and Mechanisms?

Tools of the UFR Process	Mechanisms of the UFR Process
UFR Webpage	Memorandum of Understanding Establishing the Unified Federal EHP Review Process
EHP Agency Point of Contact List	UFR Guidance for EHP Practitioners
IT Resources List	FEMA Prototype Programmatic Agreement for Section 106 of the NHPA (PPA)
EHP Disaster Recovery Skills Checklist	Template Disaster-Specific Memorandum of Understanding
Unified Federal Environmental and Historic Preservation Guide for Federal Disaster Recovery Assistance Applicants	Data Sharing Agreement Content

What is My Role in Implementing the Tools and Mechanisms?

You should understand the Tools and Mechanisms and how/when they can be used so you can:

- Educate staff about the Tools and Mechanisms and the UFR Process, such as the Practitioner Guidance.
- Recommend what Tools and Mechanisms should be used for the specific disaster event, such as the Disaster-Specific MOU.
- Identify data sharing opportunities and facilitate development of data sharing agreements to leverage other agency's resources and to better inform decisions for project planning.

How Do the Tools and Mechanisms Support Disaster Recovery?

- Tools and Mechanisms can be in place before a disaster occurs.
- Tools and Mechanisms are scalable to the needs of a particular disaster.
- Tools and Mechanisms inform the applicant in their decision making process with respect to the EHP review process.
- Tools and Mechanisms enable EHP Practitioners to share data.
- Tools and Mechanisms expedite compliance with EHP requirements.

Mechanism – UFR MOU

MOU Establishing the Unified Federal Environmental and Historic Preservation Review Process (UFR MOU)

- The UFR MOU, executed on July 29, 2014, formalizes roles and responsibilities among the 11 departments and agencies that have signed.
- The UFR MOU specifies commitments of the parties to:
    - Provide staffing and resources to support the UFR Process.
    - Distribute and use the Tools and Mechanisms.
    - Use a formalized issue elevation process to resolve disputes.

Benefit: The UFR MOU provides a commitment (for example, providing staff and resources, training, interagency communication, and oversight) to expedite EHP review for disaster recovery projects.

Click here to view the Tools and Mechanisms in the UFR Library.

Mechanism – Practitioner Guidance

UFR Guidance for EHP Practitioners (Practitioner Guidance)

- The Practitioner Guidance describes the UFR Process, the Tools and Mechanisms, and common EHP requirements that apply to disaster recovery projects. It also includes suggestions for how review may be expedited and coordinated.

Benefit: The Practitioner Guidance familiarizes EHP Practitioners with the UFR Process by connecting them with UFR Tools and Mechanisms as well as providing practical tips for implementing their role in the UFR Process.

Click here to view the Tools and Mechanisms in the UFR Library.

Mechanism – FEMA Prototype Programmatic Agreement

FEMA Prototype Programmatic Agreement for Section 106 of the NHPA (PPA)

- The PPA establishes a national model for FEMA to negotiate Section 106 state-specific programmatic agreements.
- The PPA explains when and how other federal agencies can be a signatory to the state programmatic agreement and how other federal agencies can develop their own PPA that is modeled after the FEMA PPA.

Benefit: The PPA 1) defines specific activities that have limited potential to affect historic properties and for which expedited consultation is acceptable 2) proposes pre-negotiated treatment measures to address adverse effects.

Click here to view the Tools and Mechanisms in the UFR Library.

Mechanism – Disaster-Specific MOU

Disaster-Specific MOU

- The Disaster-Specific MOU is an agreement that defines EHP roles and
  responsibilities during a specific disaster recovery effort. The template provides
  suggested topics for agreement, such as:
    - Responsibilities of parties
    - Commitments to coordinate and share information
    - Common definitions
    - Issue elevation clause

Benefit: A Disaster-Specific MOU increases communication, collaboration, and
transparency among Agencies participating in disaster recovery.

Click here to view the Tools and Mechanisms and an example disaster-specific MOU
among FEMA, NPS, and FHA for UFR of the Pu'u 'O'o Volcanic Eruption and Lava
Flow in the UFR Library.

Mechanism – Data Sharing

Data Sharing Agreement Content

- This contains a compilation of example provisions for parties to consider when
  developing data sharing agreements.

Data Standards List

- This contains a compilation of common data standards. It covers natural and
  cultural resources, general standards for GIS data, as well as federal and state
  agency-specific and resource-specific standards.

Benefits: A data sharing agreement enables the exchange of information between two or
more parties in a way that helps ensure that the parties have the same understanding of
what is being represented by the data and can exchange that information in a useful,
meaningful, and efficient way.

Click here to view the Tools and Mechanisms in the UFR Library.

Tool – UFR Webpage

UFR Webpage

- This contains resources for EHP Practitioners conducting reviews and federal assistance applicants seeking information to support EHP reviews.
- There is also a library of legal requirements and best practices.

Benefit: The UFR Webpage provides a one stop source for EHP information resources and facilitates the sharing of best practices. The website provides guidance and resources for practitioners and applicants.

Click here to view the UFR Webpage.

Tool – Agency POC List

EHP Agency Point of Contact List (Agency POC List)

- The Agency POC List has contact information organized by agency, state, disaster issue and affected resource.

Benefit: The Agency POC List provides a one stop source of information to identify appropriate POCs for EHP reviews based on disaster type and location.

Click here to view the Tools and Mechanisms in the UFR Library.

Tools – Resource and Skills Lists

IT Resources List - This is a matrix of existing IT resources (e.g., databases, decision support systems, websites, GIS mapping tools and authoritative data set sources)

EHP Disaster Recovery Skills Checklist - This is a checklist to assist the coordinating agency to identify appropriate staff to activate in support of the NCR RSF under the NDRF.

Benefits: These Tools consolidate existing data sources useful for EHP reviews and assist agencies in quickly identifying appropriate staff to activate in support of the UFR Process.

Click here to view the Tools and Mechanisms in the UFR Library.

Tool – Applicant Guide

Unified Federal Environmental and Historic Preservation Review Guide for Federal Disaster Recovery Assistance Applicants (Applicant Guide)

- The Applicant Guide contains information for applicants about EHP requirements and their role in EHP reviews.

Benefit: The Applicant Guide includes a checklist summarizing information applicants typically need to provide to funding agencies and a checklist designed to increase the likelihood of project compliance with EHP laws, regulations, and Executive orders. The checklists and tables of requirements guide applicants on their responsibilities when applying for funding from multiple agencies.

Click here to view the Tools and Mechanisms in the UFR Library.

Tool – Environmental Checklist

Template Environmental Checklist for FEMA and HUD

- This template is a list of EHP regulation requirements for FEMA and HUD responsible entities to consider when jointly funding multiple similar projects.

Benefit: This template provides a blueprint for FEMA/HUD and other agencies to standardize information to ensure that all EHP regulations are considered prior to jointly funding a project.

Click here to view the Tools and Mechanisms in the UFR Library.

Tools – Training

UFR Advisor Training (this training)

- This training is for staff who would like to obtain the UFR Advisor Specialty as well as for those individuals who may be activating as the UFR advisor.

Training for Disaster Recovery Leadership

- This is an executive level training that provides the FDRC, FCO, Recovery Office Directors and other recovery leadership with information about the UFR Process.

Benefit: The trainings explain how EHP reviews may be expedited or coordinated by disaster recovery staff. This course is a prerequisite for obtaining the UFR Advisor specialty. The leadership training supports FDRC professional development.

Click here to view the Tools and Mechanisms in the UFR Library.

Lesson 4 Summary

This lesson presented the following topics:

- Detailed descriptions
- UFR Advisor's role in implementation
- Benefits for disaster recovery

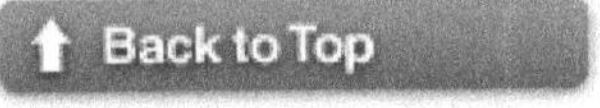

Lesson 5: Disaster Recovery Scenarios and Implementation of the UFR Process

Lesson 5: Overview

Objectives: This lesson will cover the following topics:

- Disaster Recovery Timeline
- Two disaster scenarios – annual seasonal flooding and a major hurricane

 This lesson should take approximately **30 minutes** to complete.

UFR Process During Disaster Recovery

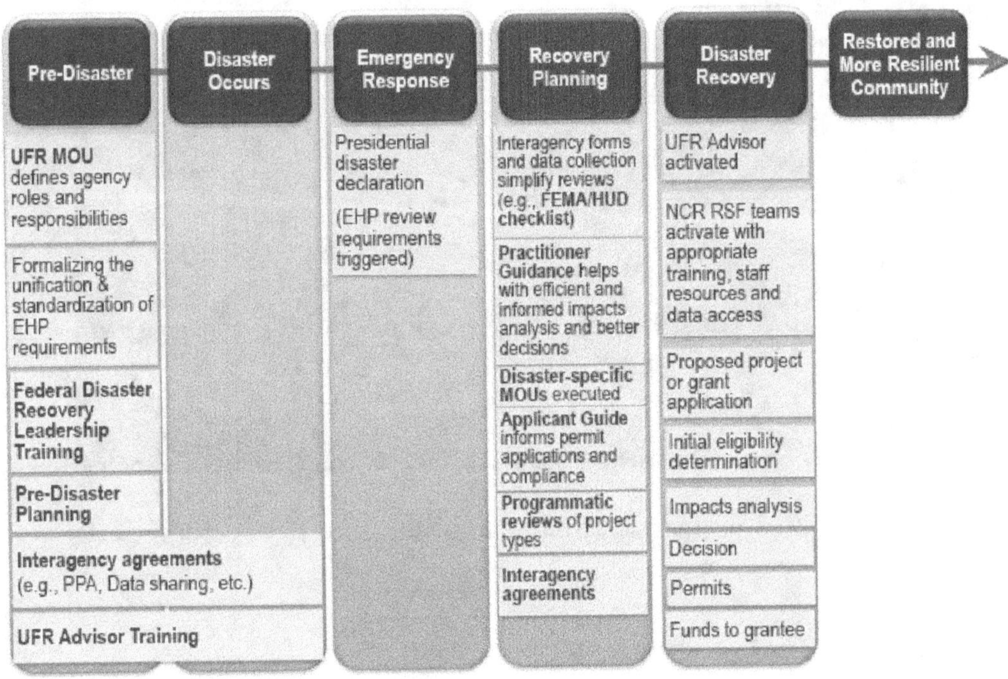

Text description of image: Timeline of the UFR Process during the phases of disaster recovery. The six phases are: 1) Pre-Disaster, 2) Disaster Occurs, 3) Emergency Response, 4) Recovery Planning, 5) Disaster Recovery, 6) Restored and More Resilient Community. During the Pre-Disaster phase, the following takes place: UFR MOU defines agency roles and responsibilities; Formalizing the unification & standardization of EHP requirements; Federal Disaster Recovery Leadership Training; and Pre-Disaster Planning. During the Pre-Disaster phase and when the Disaster Occurs, the following takes place: Interagency agreements (e.g., PPA, Data sharing, etc.) and UFR Advisor Training. During Emergency Response, the following takes place: Presidential disaster declaration (EHP review requirements triggered). During Recovery Planning, the following takes place: Interagency forms and data collection simplifies reviews (e.g., FEMA/HUD checklist); Practitioner Guidance helps EHP staff facilitate efficient and informed impacts analysis and better planning decisions; Disaster-specific MOUs executed; Applicant Guide informs permit applications and compliance; Programmatic reviews of project types; Interagency agreements. During Disaster Recovery, the following takes place: UFR Advisor activated; NCR RSF teams activate with appropriate training, staff resources and data access; Proposed project or grant application; Initial eligibility determination; Impacts analysis; Decision; Permits; Funds to grantee.

Disaster Scenario 1: Annual Seasonal Flooding

Photo of aftermath of July 2013 in Bannack State Park, Montana (photo credit Carl Davis, U.S. Forest Service).

Annual Seasonal Flooding: Disaster Overview

The event:

- Warm spring temperatures in Montana
- Heavy rain and wind from spring thunderstorms
- Small scale flooding
- Exceeds capacity of state and local government
- Results in a presidential disaster declaration

Agencies involved:

- Department of Transportation (DOT), FEMA, HUD, Advisory Council on Historic Preservation
- State agencies

Other factors:

- FDRC appointed and activated
- 2-3 RSFs are activated
- UFR Advisor is activated

Workers divert creek to begin repairs on bridge (photo credit HUD)

Annual Seasonal Flooding: Pre-Disaster

- **UFR MOU** commitments recognized
- Interagency group developed to:
    - Share EHP compliance information.
    - Develop **Programmatic Environmental Assessments.**
    - Share **Practitioner Guidance**
- **Data sharing agreements** established
    - Share data among participants: FEMA, HUD, DOT, Montana Department of Transportation, Montana Department of Natural Resources, etc.
- The **REO** and **Regional UFR Coordinator** coordinate pre-disaster planning.

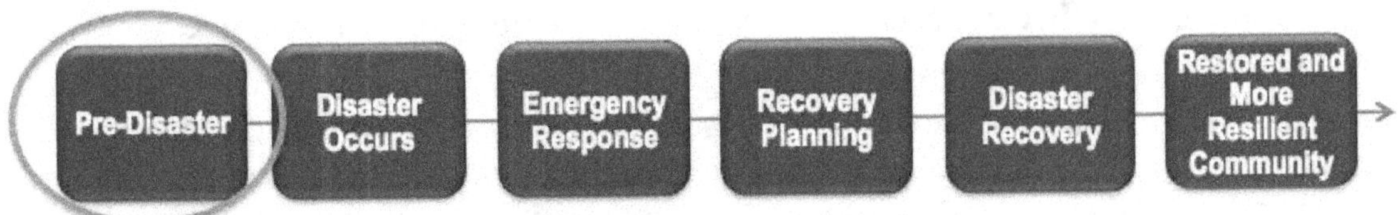

Annual Seasonal Flooding: Recovery Planning

- The UFR Advisor conducts a UFR **Mission Scoping Assessment** and identifies a UFR mission based on necessary interagency coordination during disaster recovery.
- Local and state agencies, including the Montana Department of Transportation, identify potential projects.
- FEMA, HUD, DOT and the Montana Department of Health use the **Practitioner Guidance** to identify ways to expedite EHP reviews.

Click here to view the Tools and Mechanisms in the UFR Library.

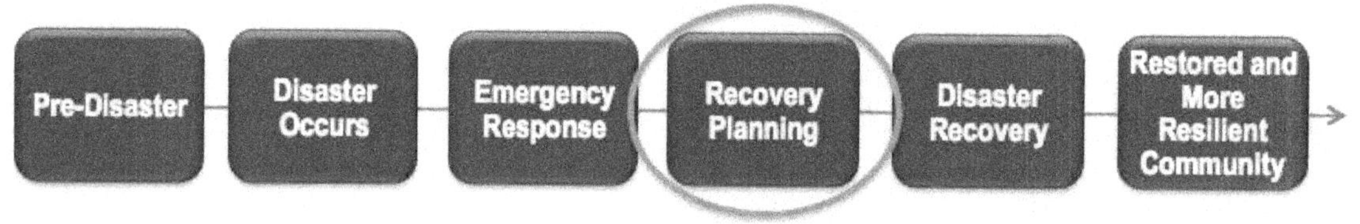

Annual Seasonal Flooding: Disaster Recovery

- FEMA / HUD joint funding
- Using the **Template Checklist for FEMA/HUD**
- Identify other agencies who may benefit from signing on to the PPA
- Identify opportunities to tier off from existing **Programmatic Environmental Assessments**

Click here to view the Tools and Mechanisms in the UFR Library.

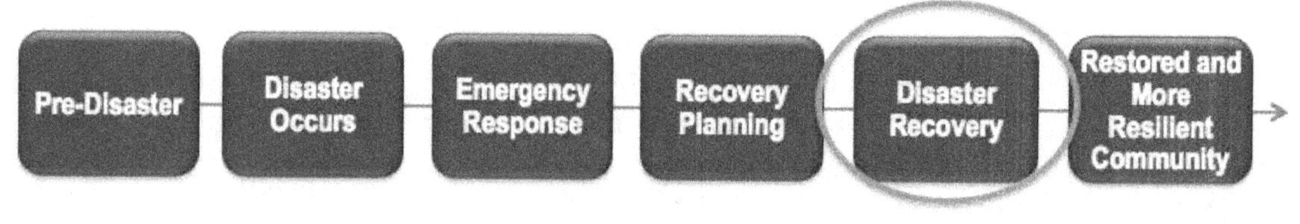

EHP Review With and Without the UFR Process - *Section 106 Consultation*

Before the UFR Process	**Under the UFR Process**
Prior to the FEMA Prototype Programmatic Agreement (PPA), FEMA and other Federal agencies (OFA) independently analyzed the project's potential to affect	When executed, the PPA allows OFA to sign onto the PPA in order to utilize the agreement to satisfy their Section 106 responsibilities when appropriate. This

historic properties using separate processes/programmatic approaches.

Agency and State/Tribal Historic Preservation Office (SHPO/THPO) staff time was spent identifying, evaluating, and assessing effects of projects that would have No Effect or No Adverse Effect on historic properties.

FEMA and OFAs separately identified and evaluated historic properties for the NRHP and submitted its findings to SHPO and/or THPO for concurrence. The federal agency made a determination of effects on the historic properties.

allows the OFA to utilize the same benefits and efficiencies offered to FEMA.

PPA establishes an abbreviated process to streamline activities that have no effects historic properties, thus avoiding the lengthy review time.

FEMA and OFA will identify opportunities to coordinate Section 106 reviews for jointly funded projects, thus reducing duplication of effort and overburdening the SHPO/THPO.

How the UFR Process Enhanced Disaster Recovery

Text description of image: Diagram of two text boxes: one listing Tools/Mechanisms used during disaster connected with an arrow pointing to the other text box that lists Benefits of the UFR Process, illustrating that benefits arise from the use of the Tools and Mechanisms. The Tools and Mechanisms used during the disaster include: - Programmatic Environmental Assessment; - Data Sharing Agreements; - Practitioner Guidance; - PPA; and - Template Checklist for FEMA/HUD. The benefits of the UFR Process include: - Expedited federal determinations for disaster recovery projects; - Consistency and coordination among various agency environmental and historic preservation reviews; - Leveraged and efficient use of agency staff and funds; - Quick resolution of coordination challenges; and - More informed federal decision making.

Disaster Scenario 2: Major Hurricane

Photo of an aerial view of damage caused by the storm surge of Hurricane Sandy on the coastline of New York, Nov. 2012 (photo credit Jocelyn Augustino, FEMA)

Major Hurricane: Disaster Overview

The event:

- Mass evacuations and record floods in NY and NJ
- Utility infrastructure is damaged
- Debris accumulates
- Sensitive environmental areas impacted
- Homes destroyed
- Presidential disaster declaration

Agencies involved:

- DOT, FEMA, HUD, U.S. Army Corps of Engineers (USACE), tribes and state and local governments

Other factors:

- FDRC appointed and activated
- RSFs are activated
- UFR Advisor is activated

Photo of Breezy Point, New York after Hurricane Sandy
storm surges and related fire ravaged the
neighborhood, Oct. 2012 (photo credit FEMA)

Major Hurricane: Pre-Disaster

- **UFR MOU** commitments recognized
- Section 106 programmatic agreement established using the **PPA**.
- **ESA Matrix** and how-to-guide developed: National Oceanic and Atmospheric
  Administration (NOAA), US Fish and Wildlife Service (FWS), HUD, USACE
  and DOT have signed.
- The **REO** and **Regional UFR Coordinator** coordinate pre-disaster planning.

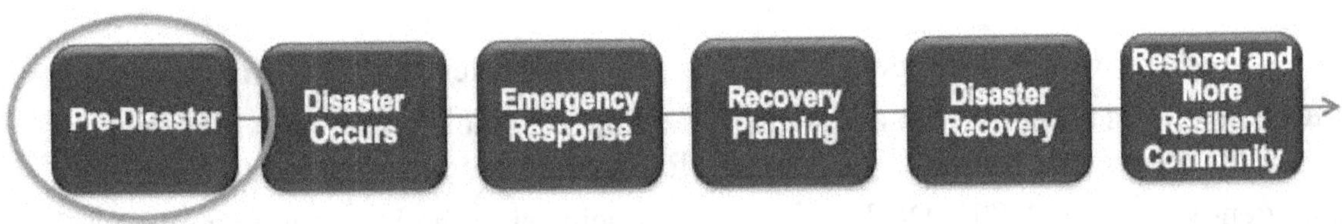

Major Hurricane: Recovery Planning

UFR Advisor assists parties to develop a **Disaster-Specific MOU** for:

- Consultation timelines
- Agency roles and responsibilities
- Meeting coordination
- Agency points of contact

Click here to view the Tools and Mechanisms in the UFR Library.

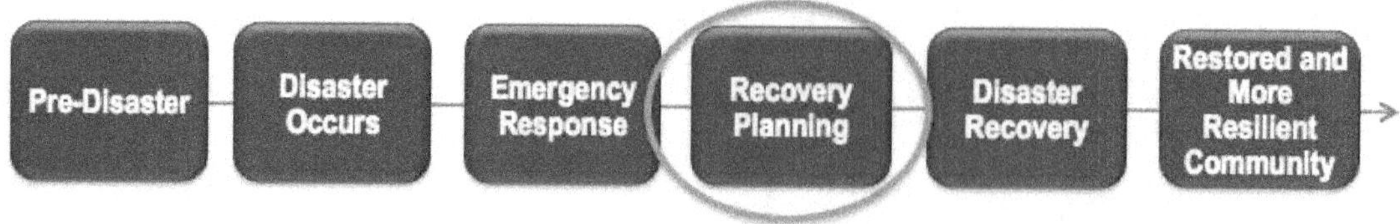

Major Hurricane: Disaster Recovery

- Agencies share the **Applicant Guide** at applicant briefings.
- EHP Practitioners inform applicants of agency specific requirements and coordinating joint funding timelines.
- Applicants provide the necessary information for agencies to conduct the EHP reviews.
- Applicants notify funding agencies of joint funding requests.

Click here to view the Tools and Mechanisms in the UFR Library.

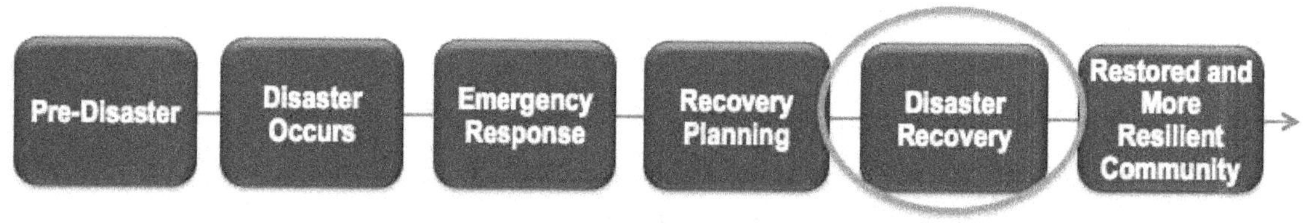

EHP Review With and Without the UFR Process - *Coordination of Agencies – Section 7 Consultation*

Before the UFR Process	Under the UFR Process
Multiple agencies respond with assistance for disaster recovery efforts.	Multiple agencies respond with assistance for disaster recovery efforts.
Each agency (FEMA, HUD, DOT, etc.) independently completes EHP review (including consultation with National Marine Fisheries Service (NMFS)/FWS.	Agencies sign the Disaster-Specific MOU which identifies recovery project priorities, information sharing opportunities and roles and responsibilities of each agency.
Applicants/agencies collect data/information about the species that could be affected and the effect of their project on the species.	Using the Practitioner Guidance agencies share data / project information. The ESA Matrix is used to quickly assess species impacts.
NMFS/FWS are overwhelmed with requests from multiple agencies concurrently.	Agencies coordinate on ESA consultations by submitting a joint consultation request to NMFS/FWS.
Federal agency effort may be duplicated. Staff resources may not be focused on the highest priority projects for recovery.	Reduced duplication of agency effort, allowing for determinations to be made quicker. Agencies share

information/perspective on the projects improving the decision making. Highest priority projects are expedited.

EHP Review With and Without the UFR Process - *Coordination of Agencies – NEPA*

Before the UFR Process	**Under the UFR Process**
Multiple agencies respond with assistance for disaster recovery efforts.	Multiple agencies respond with assistance for disaster recovery efforts.
Each agency independently completes EHP review for its own assistance programs and projects including compliance with NEPA.	Agencies sign the Disaster-Specific MOU which identifies information sharing opportunities and roles and responsibilities of each agency. Applicants notify agencies of joint funding efforts allowing them to better align NEPA timing and analyses.
Applicants/funding agencies collect data/information about the projects and analyze the effect of their project on the environment.	Agencies share data and project information and also coordinate analysis needs for related projects.
Agencies complete their own NEPA analyses on separate timelines and using different levels of NEPA analysis.	Coordination of analysis requirements for related projects allows one agency to adopt another agency's NEPA analysis.
Federal agency effort may be duplicated. Applicants await the results of multiple overlapping NEPA analyses before proceeding with their project.	Reduced duplication of agency effort, allowing for determinations to be made quicker. Agencies share information/perspective on the projects improving the decision making.

How the UFR Process Enhanced Disaster Recovery

Tools/Mechanisms used during disaster:

- PPA
- ESA Matrix
- Disaster-Specific MOU
- Applicant Guide

Benefits of UFR Process:

- Expedited federal determinations for disaster recovery projects
- Consistency and coordination among various agency EHP reviews
- Leveraged and efficient use of agency staff and funds
- Quick resolution of coordination challenges
- More informed federal decision making

Text description of image: Diagram of two text boxes: one listing Tools/Mechanisms used during disaster connected with an arrow pointing to the other text box that lists Benefits of the UFR Process, illustrating that benefits arise from the use of the Tools and Mechanisms. The Tools and Mechanisms used during the disaster include: - PPA; - ESA Matrix; - Disaster-Specific MOU; and - Applicant Guide. The benefits of the UFR Process include: - Expedited federal determinations for disaster recovery projects; - Consistency and coordination among various agency EHP reviews; - Leveraged and efficient use of agency staff and funds; - Quick resolution of coordination challenges; and - More informed federal decision making.

Lesson 5 Summary

This lesson presented the following topics:

- Disaster Recovery Timeline
- Two disaster scenarios – annual seasonal flooding and a major hurricane

Lesson 6: Course Summary

Lesson 6: Overview

Objectives: The purpose of this lesson is to:

- Review the key concepts presented in this course
- Prepare for taking the final exam

 This lesson should take approximately **10 minutes** to complete.

Review – Lesson 2: The UFR Process and Interagency Coordination

Establishment: The Sandy Recovery Improvement Act of 2013 required development of an expedited process for EHP reviews following disasters and the UFR MOU formally established the UFR Process.

The UFR Process is integrated with the **NDRF** and the **IRC**.

Applicability: The UFR Process applies whenever multiple agencies are engaged in similar disaster recovery efforts following a presidentially declared disaster.

Benefits: The UFR Process improves coordination, reduces duplication of effort, leverages existing agreements, and aligns multiple agency review processes.

Review – Lesson 3: The UFR Advisor

Role: The UFR Advisor is the interagency coordinator for EHP compliance who educates staff about the UFR Process and recommends Tools and Mechanisms to support disaster recovery.

Activation: After a disaster occurs and an FDRC is appointed, the UFR Advisor activates. The nature of further UFR Advisor responsibilities depends on the outcome of the Mission Scoping Assessment. If an FDRC is not appointed, an EHP Advisor may request the assistance of a staff member with the UFR specialty within the EHP cadre.

Interface: The UFR Advisor works with the National and Regional UFR Coordinators, the FEMA Regional Environmental Officer, Recovery Support Function Field Coordinators, the FEMA EHP Advisor, and Disaster Recovery Leadership.

Review – Lesson 4: Tools and Mechanisms of the UFR Process

The Tools and Mechanisms expedite EHP reviews by addressing gaps, increasing consistency, and leveraging existing resources.

Tools	**Mechanisms**
UFR Webpage	UFR MOU
Agency POC List	Practitioner Guidance
IT Resources List	FEMA Prototype Programmatic Agreement
EHP Disaster Recovery Skills Checklist	Disaster-Specific MOU
Applicant Guide	Data Sharing
Template Environmental Checklist	
Training	

Review – Lesson 5: Disaster Recovery Scenarios and Implementation of the UFR Process

The UFR Tools and Mechanisms are used both before a disaster occurs and throughout the recovery planning and recovery processes.

The UFR Tools and Mechanisms can be applied to multiple stages of disaster recovery efforts.

The UFR Process can expedite Section 106 Consultation, Section 7 Consultation, and NEPA analysis as well as other regulatory requirements.

Lesson 6 Summary

You have now completed the overview of the UFR Process and the role of the UFR Advisor.

As you perform the duties of this position, remember that your primary responsibility is to coordinate EHP compliance across federal agencies, provide expertise for the implementation of the UFR Process, and determine what specific Tools and Mechanisms are going to be used for the specific disaster event to further EHP compliance as part of the UFR Process.